Words for the Soul

Rahat. A. Malik

BookLeaf
Publishing

India | USA | UK

Presentation by *BookLeaf Publishing*

Web: www.bookleafpub.com

E-mail: info@bookleafpub.com

ISBN : 9789357448765

First edition 2021

DEDICATION

Dedicated to my family whose support is
priceless. Much Love X

ACKNOWLEDGEMENT

All praise to the Lord of the Worlds who created
me from a piece of flesh and gave me life.
Please accept my humble efforts.

PREFACE

Life is not a walk in the park, we all are going through our inner struggles, though there is one thing which will prevail- belief in the Almighty. These are my mere thoughts which I hope will assist others in going through their hardships.

Remember kindness, politeness, positive, support costs nothing. As the Prophet pbuh said, 'Be kind, for whenever kindness becomes part of something it beautifies it.'

Ya Allah

Ya Allah,

I am broken,

Help me!
Love your humble servant.

Hope

You are the light within the darkness,
You are the hope when one is hopeless,
You are the giver when one has nothing,
You are the healer when souls are in despair,
You are the compassionate when hard
heartedness is rife,
You are the guardian when one feels alone,
You are the ultimate witness when people are
wronged,
You are the strength when people are weak,
You are the guide when we've lost our way,
You are the first,
You are the last,
The Almighty,
The Omnipotent,
The Exalted,
To you goes all praise,
Hope.

Believe

So he invoked his Lord, 'Indeed I am
overpowered so help.'

Believe with every bone in your body,
Every breath you've ever taken,
Every tear you have every cried,
Every drop of blood you've ever shed,
Every time your heart is broken,
Every time you've felt like giving up,
Every time someone has wronged you,
Every time you feel alone,
Every time you feel no one is listening,
He is the one,
Only,
Healer of hearts,
Giver of peace and solidarity,
He is One!

My Lord do not leave me alone.

Iqra

Read in the name of your Lord,
Stop,
Ponder,
Reflect,
As the sun splashes it rays over the expansive
sky,
When the thunder furiously rolls,
The flash of lighting as it lights up the sky,
The birds as they search for food at dawn,
Why the two seas meet but never mix,
Nothing is created without reason,
Sit and think,
You are one of 7.9 billion,
You are one of his beloved creations
Read.

Sabr

Patience is paining,
Heart wrenching,
Soul crushing,
But your Lord does not waste the pain of the
patient one,
He is all seeing,
All hearing,
He knows it is hard,
At times intolerable,
But remember,
He does not burden a soul beyond which it can
bear
You will be rewarded,
Be hopeful,
After darkness there is light,
After night there is day,
At the end of a tunnel there is space,
Moments of hardship don't last forever,
You will gain more than you have ever lost,
Sabr.

The Throne

The first creation,
The greatest of things,
The grandeur is breathtaking,
Size is incomprehensible,
Positioned above water,
Towering above,
Huge angels bearing it with pride,
Mighty and strong,
It has emblazoned on it,
'My mercy overpowers My anger.'
Take hope,
The Throne.

A Moment of Solitude

A moment of solitude can be quite refreshing,
Sitting and thinking is really quite the blessing,
Though you may feel alone, you truly are not,
Angels on your shoulders, write.....though you
may have forgot.
They give you a chance to correct your ways,
Wait six hours for you to repent and pray,
If you sit and reflect,
Observe your surroundings,
So much to be grateful for,
Lighting strikes and thunder rolls...all so
astounding.
Your Lord has created nothing without reason,
You and me, birds and the bees,
All included in the entirety of his completion.

An Nisa

The woman,
The lady,
The girl,
The sister,
The mother,
The aunt,
The grandmother
Created from a rib,
Companion,
An equal,
Paradise at her feet,
Queen of the home,
Educators,
Scholars,
Scientists,
List is endless,
Dreamers,
Writers,
Traders,
Improving,
Serving,
Leading,
A pillar of the community
Dignified and honoured
Precious,
An Nisa

Recite

SubhanAllah
Alhamdulilah
Allahu Akhbar
Till your last breath
There is none worthy of worship except Allah
and Muhammed (pbuh) is the messenger of
Allah.
Think

CTRL+ ALT+ DEL

Control your speech,
Alter your tone,
Delete aggressive language.

Ode to God

To describe you would do no justice.
Your greatness is superior
To you belong all the best words
The riches of every living and non-living thing
We are in awe of your creations
How the wind blows
How the seas meet but never mix
How life was created
How you know what is in every heart
We submit
Saying there is no God but you.

In Need

You break me to build me
You take to give me
You make me worry to appreciate blessings
You give me hardships to develop me
You make me feel like a stranger to bring me
closer to you
Everything starts with you and ends with you
Please take me into your protection and do not
leave me for a blink of an eye.

We Submit

When the thunder rolls and lighting strikes
When the birds tweet at dawn
The sun prostrates to you before it rises
Fishes in the depths of the vast ocean
The looming mountains
The twinkling stars
Humans and beasts
Everything submits
In awe of your greatness
You are divine
The First and last
Accept our worship

Hope

Sometimes in the most helpless moment
When your heart is breaking
Shattering
You feel like giving up
Falling
Weak
Grieving
Your Lord will reveal
A blessing
Or many
A friend
An aide
A skill
A tool
That you never knew existed
Because when HE takes he always gives
something greater.
Hope

Reward

Never forget for every pain you feel
You will be rewarded
For every tear you shed
You will be rewarded
For every heartbreak you receive
You will be rewarded
For every time you have been wronged
You will be rewarded
For every time you sacrifice
You will be rewarded
You every time to do anything to please God
You will be rewarded.

99

The compassionate
The merciful
The king
The holy
The source of peace and safety
The guarantor
The guardian
The almighty
The irresistible
The majestic
The creator
The designer
The fashioner of forms
The repeatedly forgiving
The subduer
The bestower
The provider
The victory giver
The all knowing
The restrainer
The extender
The abaser
The exalted
The giver of honour

The giver of dishonour
The all hearing
The all seeing
The judge
The utterly just
The gentle
The aware
The forbearing
The magnificent
The much-forgiving
The grateful
The sublime
The great
The preserver
The nourisher
The bringer of judgement
The majestic
The bountiful
The watchful
The responsive
The vast
The wise
The loving
The glorious
The resurrecter
The witness
The truth
The trustee
The strong

The firm
The friend, patron and helper
The all praiseworthy
The numberer of all
The orginator
The reinstater
the giver of life
The destroyer
The living
The guardian
The perceiver
The illustrious
The unique
The indivisable
The eternal
The omnipotent
The determiner
The expediter
He who puts far away
The first
The last
The manifest
The hidden
The patron
The exalted
The good
The ever returning
The avenger
The pardoner

The kind
The owner of sovereignty
The lord of majesty and generosity
The equitable
The gatherer
The independent
The enricher
The withholder
The distressor
The source of good
The light
The guide
The incomparable
The immutable
The inheritor of all
The guide to the right path
The timeless

Roaming

Roaming through the streets on an Winter's day
Meandering through the park when the
Autumnal leaves fall
Gazing at the endless ocean on a Summer's day
Waking up to birds tweeting on a Spring
morning
These are his miracles
Therefore why do we fear when life does not go
our way
Believe in the one who split the moon in two
Split the Red Sea
Protected in three layers of darkness
Cooled the fire
We become hopeless
Impatient
He is the giver of miracles
We just have to believe
He has not left us
He is waiting for us to return.

Alone or Not?

When the day comes to a close
The light turns into darkness
When people scurry home
When the pace slows down
Darkness envelops the sky
The moon shines its brightest
The stars twinkle in the night sky
You may feel alone
Thinking who is around to hear your woes
See your tears fall
Wonder who will catch you when you fall
There is a being
Better than all
Who wants you to call out to HIM
Who wants to listen to your every word
He is the best possible listener
The best possible aide
He is One.

Pray

Pray with every bone in your body
Pray when you are crying an endless ocean of
tears
Pray when you are weak and fragile
Pray when you have only an ounce of energy left
Pray when your feel there is no hope
Pray when you everyone has turned their back to
you
Pray when you feel alone in a crowded room
Pray when you have been ostracised
You are praying to the Lord of the Worlds
He is the giver of miracles
Know he does not take but only to give ten fold
He rewards you even you received a prick of a
thorn
The only being who knows what's in your heart
without you saying it
Pray with your last breath.
He only says,'Ku Fa Ya Koon.'

Ya Allah V2

Ya Allah
I believe

Accept what I offer.
Love your humble servant.

www.ingramcontent.com/pod-product-compliance
Lightning Source LLC
LaVergne TN
LVHW021719210726
843509LV00021B/2858